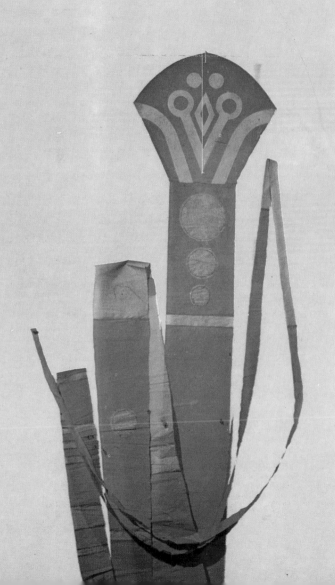

A Panda Paperback

CONTENTS

The author, Jean-Paul
Mouvier, is 29 years old.
He is a great kite enthusiast
and the kites he has selected
in this book are all highly
unusual and extremely
colorful without being too
difficult to make.

Drawings by the author
Photos by
Sophie Laverrière
Louis Beetchen
Giraudon
Japanese Tourist Office
Musée de l'Air in Paris.

Text and illustrations
© 1974 Editions Gallimard
© 1974 English language edition
Franklin Watts, Inc., New York, N.Y.
Printed in France

SBN : 531-02422-9
Library of Congress Catalog Card
Number : 73-14005

KITES!

FRANKLIN WATTS, INC.
NEW YORK, N.Y. 1974

The author

3

Kites and their origins

Kites first came into being in China and were found all over Asia and the islands of the Pacific from an early date.

Kites as objects of worship

Kites originally had a definite religious significance and function related to the spirits or deities worshiped in those countries. Many of these early religious traditions and practices still survive. In Indonesia the kites that fishermen and sailors fly from their canoes are regarded as symbols of the human soul and of the victory of the spiritual over the physical aspect of man's existence. In Polynesia kites represent different deities or carry the emblems of mighty chieftains. In Cambodia it was customary to fly a kite with a strip of bamboo attached to it above the house at night. The bamboo would give off a strange plaintive sound as it vibrated in the wind, and this was supposed to frighten away evil spirits. At the beginning of each New Year, Korean families write the name and date of birth of each of their sons on a kite. Once the kite is high in the air, they cut the line so that the kite is carried a long way off, thus enticing the evil spirits away from the children whose names are inscribed on it. A similar tradition exists among the Vietnamese, who, as part of their New Year celebrations, hang as many wind-socks outside their house as there are boys in the family.

4

Kites come to Europe

Kites were first introduced into Europe in the fifteenth century by English, Dutch, and Portuguese merchants. They were still comparatively rare in the sixteenth century, but by the seventeenth century had become very fashionable and were playing a spectacular part in many major celebrations and firework displays. Sometimes a dragon kite was filled with gunpowder so that it exploded in midair, or a lozenge kite would be flown with streamers and bangers attached to the tail. As a child Sir Isaac Newton had a passion for kites. He used to terrify local farmers by fastening a lantern to his kite at night and using it to light his way.

Kites in wartime

The earliest record of the use of kites in a military context concerns a Chinese general, Han-Sin, who in the year 196 B.C. used a kite to calculate the distance between his army and the palace he was besieging; he was thus able to dig a tunnel under the palace walls and take its inhabitants by surprise. Kites came to be used increasingly for military purposes, for signaling or for establishing contact between different sections of the same army over a long distance. They were sometimes fitted with whistles and lanterns and flown over the enemy camp at dead of night. The eerie sounds and flickering lights often proved more effective in intimidating the enemy than a show of arms in broad daylight. During the Civil War troops used kites to distribute adverse propaganda behind the enemy lines.

Kites were used in a less official capacity to smuggle alcohol into Paris in 1870 when the city was besieged by the Prussians.

"Why, it's a kite!"

"It can't be! Yes, it is...a whole lot of monks playing with kites!"

Above: *Captain Haddock, Tintin's faithful friend, comes across kites in China.*
Below: *The American cartoon hero Charlie Brown wrestling with a particularly vicious kite.*
Opposite: *A famous painting entitled* La Cometa, *by the Spanish artist Goya.*

Kite games and kite fights

About 1825, George Pocock, an English schoolmaster from Bristol, had the ingenious idea of substituting the horses of his horse-drawn carriage with a train of kites, thereby creating the first ever "kite-drawn" carriage. This remarkable vehicle carried Pocock and his friends over distances of more than a hundred miles across the English countryside and evoked considerable comment on the way. In particularly favorable conditions it once reached the record speed of 30 mph.

In 1903 an American kite enthusiast named Cody succeeded in sailing across the English Channel in a small boat towed along by a kite. A countryman of his, Benjamin Franklin, had apparently used the same technique of attaching his boat to a kite when he was a small boy. A kite-drawn vehicle in the water or on dry land can provide hours of fun. Or, if you are feeling like something a little more aggressive, why not challenge your friends to a kite fight? Kites still play a very important part in major festivities all over Asia. During the three months of the spring when the wind is blowing in the right direction, the whole population of Thailand takes part in a series of traditional kite fights. Two teams challenge each other: on one side are the female **papkaos,** light, easily maneuverable kites with tails, and on the other the male **chulas,** strong, slow-moving kites without a tail. The papkaos are armed with rope lassos and the chulas with bunches of bamboo strips tied to the kite line. Each team endeavors to trap and entangle the enemy with the weapons at their disposal. In China and in Korea, part of the handline is covered with little pieces of cut glass, and the contestants then try to slice through each other's lines using a sawing motion.

A kite fight on the banks of the Kariyata River in Japan.

Some facts about

The first human ascents

According to an ancient Japanese legend, a famous thief by the name of Ishikawa once made a daring attempt to steal the golden dolphins from the top of the tower of a nearby castle. One moonless night he attached himself to an enormous kite and, with the aid of his sons, managed to rise into the air until he was hovering above the tower. But fate was against him; he managed to snatch the fins of the dolphins only. Later his crime was discovered and he and his entire family were boiled in oil.

The earliest man-lifting kites were, however, Chinese. History records a ban on extra-large kites issued in the reign of an early Chinese emperor who had been told that he would lose his throne to a foreign usurper descending from the heavens. The first written evidence of a human ascent is provided by the enterprising schoolmaster George Pocock, who in 1830 records having sent

Soldiers lining up a train of "observation" kites, which will take a man up into the air.

his daughter up to a height of three hundred feet. She was seated in a chair, which was then fastened to the kite.

Baden-Powell's experiments with kites aroused a great deal of popular interest. On June 27, 1894, he himself went up ten feet in a basket attached to a hexagonal kite with a wingspan of 36 feet. The following year, realizing the possible dangers of using a single kite for this type of venture, he built the *Levitor*, a string of four hexagonal kites that enabled him to go up as far as one hundred feet.

About 1900 the American Cody succeeded in lifting a man up the handline, using a string of kites and the messenger principle. The passenger was able to control his ascent with a braking system; he was equipped with a camera and a telephone linking him to the ground, and on this occasion reached the record height of four thousand feet.

By 1910 kite ascents were

becoming increasingly popular all over Europe and in the United States. Clubs of kite enthusiasts were being formed in a number of different countries, and in 1913 an international kite contest was held at Spa in Belgium. Despite a rather mild wind, numerous successful ascents were made in the course of a single afternoon.

At the beginning of the First World War, the British, French, Italian, and Russian armies all formed special kite units using kites for the purposes of enemy observation. With the subsequent rapid developments in aviation, the kite was soon replaced by hot-air balloons and, eventually, by airplanes. Meanwhile the Germans were using kites for reconnaissance at sea from submarines. A man was hoisted up the handline in a basket by means of a winch. The problem of bringing the man down rapidly in case of emergency was solved by placing the man inside the kite itself. In this way, if the submarine was forced to submerge suddenly, the man could cut the cable and, by

Observation kites. Note the two different types of kite used.

12

shifting his position, convert the kite into a glider. During the Second World War the Germans once again took up the idea of aerial reconnaissance from submarines, this time using a kite equipped with three propeller blades, closely resembling a helicopter. This machine was also widely used in the distribution of propaganda.

For some years now a certain number of daring enthusiasts in different parts of Europe have been flying with the aid of huge kites attached to their bodies and arms. They take off from clifftops or are pulled along by a car until they gather enough speed to be able to glide along in the air making use of rising currents to buoy them up. But these acrobatic feats are extremely dangerous and the slightest mistake can easily cost the men their lives.

**The kite's contribution
to modern aviation**

From
kites
to airplanes

Many of the early
pioneers in the field of
aviation in the nineteenth
century must have toyed
with the idea of fastening an
engine to a kite and using it
to drive a propeller that would
spin around in the air like
a ship's propeller in water.

The first man to succeed
in putting this idea into
effect was Clément Ader.
On October 9, 1890, he
launched the "Eole," a
motor-powered,
"heavier-than-air" machine.
It flew only about 165 feet
before coming down to
earth again, but this short
flight was to mark the
beginning of a whole new era.

Meanwhile, in the United
States, the Wright brothers
were experimenting with
different types of gliders. On
December 17, 1903, Orville
Wright took off from Kitty
Hawk in a kite-glider
equipped with a sixteen-
horsepower engine and two
propellers.

Airplanes now are
capable of flying at twice
the speed of sound, and in
this modern space age, the
contribution that kites made
to one of the major
inventions of all time is
often forgotten.

Kites and science

In June, 1752, Benjamin
Franklin used kites fitted
with projecting metal spikes
and cables to study different
aspects of atmospheric
electricity. His research in
this field was to lead to his
invention of the lightning
conductor.

In the nineteenth and early
twentieth centuries a great
number of meteorological
observations were made with
the aid of kites: atmospheric
temperature readings,
measurements of wind
velocity and of humidity,
aerial photographs for
surveying purposes. The
maximum height recorded
was on August 1, 1919, when
a string of eight kites roses to
31,000 feet in the United
States.

In 1906 kites were used to
take aerial photographs to
help determine the extent of
the damage caused by the
great San Francisco
earthquake. They are still
extensively used today in
photographing archaeological
sites from the air and in
surveying large areas.

The large kite shown above is called a **delta plane.** It works on a very simple principle. To take off, the flier runs in the direction from which the wind is blowing. To make the kite rise he simply pushes the bar away from him and to bring it down again he pulls the bar towards him. The delta plane is very easy to manipulate and can be used equally well for short and long flights depending on how long the person wishes to stay in the air. This invention has become extremely popular in the United States.

Advice
to kite
fliers

All kites are made up of
a frame and a sail, and some
of them also have a tail. The
kite is fastened by means of a
bridle to a handline, which
is wound around a reel held
in the flier's hand.

Materials: Pencils, ruler,
drafting triangle, scissors,
sharp knife, cellulose glue,
rolls of adhesive tape and
cellophane tape, sewing
needle, spool of cotton
thread, some linen thread,
a ball of thin twine (sold in
hardware stores and
stationers).

The sail is usually made of
paper. Pages of a notebook,
newspaper, crepe paper,
kraft, plain or decorated
wrapping paper, or
lightweight drawing paper.
Some sails are made of
fabric; use turkey red cotton,
an inexpensive lightweight
cotton that comes in a
variety of bright colors.
Cloth sails have the advantage
of being much stronger than
paper ones, which tend to
tear after a little use. This

means that they can be made
on a very large scale; they
do, however, need to be
machine - rather than
hand-stitched and should
not be attempted without a
sewing machine.

All sorts of different forms
of decoration are possible.
You can use a felt-tip pen
or watercolor paints, or
stick pieces of glossy paper,
aluminum foil, or any other
lightweight colored paper
onto the sail for decoration.
(Avoid using crepe paper
because it cannot be glued
very satisfactorily.)

You can make very
attractive transparencies by
cutting out little windows in
the sail and sticking tracing
paper or transparent colored
candy wrappers behind
them. These show up
particularly well when
the kite is in the air with
the sun behind it. If you
want to make sure that
your decoration is
symmetrical, cut out all the
pieces of paper that are
to be stuck onto the sail in
double thickness. This is
much simpler and saves time.

A few words of advice
when you begin designing
your own models: if you
want to make a bird or an
insect, have a good look at
a picture of one first. Never
use more than three colors
for any one kite. Too many
colors spoil the effect. If your
kite has a tail, make it in

one of the colors you have chosen for the sail. Once you have finished your kite, reinforce the underneath of the sail by sticking small rectangular pieces of paper over any weak points–such as reflex angles or the

Reinforcing the frame.

points where the bridle is fastened to the sail.

Making your own pattern

Each square on the special grid diagrams represents 2 inches. The sail is always shown in color, the frame in black, and the points at which the bridle should be attached are marked by white crosses. In the description of the different kite sticks, the first figure always represents the width and the second figure the thickness.

Make the pattern for your kite by reproducing *half* the grid diagram to its correct size. To do this, make your own grid with 2-inch squares and copy the outline of the kite onto it by counting the number of squares it occupies.

Cut out the pattern and place it on the sheet of paper you have chosen for the sail. Fold the paper in half first. Cut out the sail, using the pattern as a guide (as in dressmaking). Use the same procedure for cutting out the different parts of the decoration. Draw the decoration on the paper pattern first. Cut it out and transfer each part to the paper you want to use, again folded in half. Cut out all the elements and stick them to the sail.

Detailed instructions have been given concerning the particular pattern, type of paper, and frame to use for each kite. You can, however, alter the size of the kite if you want to, provided you keep in mind the two most essential characteristics of a kite:

Weight: The smaller the kite, the thinner the paper should be (crepe paper or newspaper), and the less decoration there should be on it. Thick paper and large designs stuck on for decoration should be reserved for the bigger kites.

Balance: All kites must be perfectly symmetrical to the right and left of their vertical axes. Nonsymmetrical kites can be made so that they balance perfectly, but this is a tricky business and takes a great deal of time.

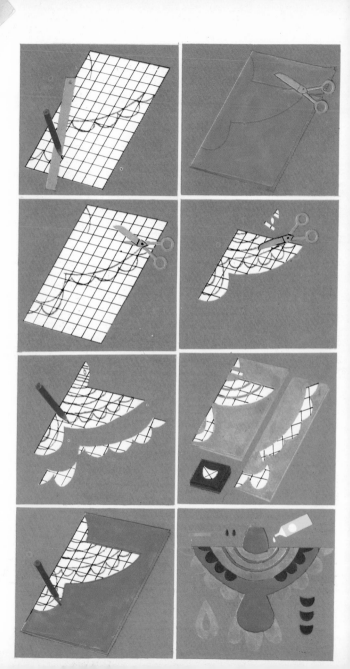

All the kites described in this book are straightforward and simple both to make and to fly.

The frame is made of lengths of bamboo or reed (sold in gardening shops for making garden props or stakes). Small poplar twigs make good sticks for the smaller models. Branches of hazel, poplar, willow, chestnut, and ash can also be used provided they are nice and straight and perfectly dry (always dry them *out* of the sun). The size of the frame varies according to the size of the kite. The large models need whole- or half-width bamboos and the smaller ones quarter-widths. To make these smaller sticks, take a cane of bamboo that is approximately 1 inch in diameter and split it down the middle, using a knife. Each piece can be split once more, according to the width and thickness of stick you need. Smooth off any rough edges or knots on the inside, but do not touch the shiny outside.

A word of warning: The cut edges of the bamboo are sharp. Protect the thumb and forefinger holding the stick with a piece of adhesive tape.

Balance: The horizontal sticks must always be perfectly balanced. Test them by marking the center with a pencil and balancing the stick on the blade of a knife. The vertical kite sticks should be slightly heavier at the bottom than at the top. Test them in the same way.

Once you have finished the frame, hold it up by the bridle so that it hangs horizontally. It should not tilt at all in relation to its vertical axis. If it is not perfectly balanced, weight the lighter side accordingly.

Diagrams opposite: *Making your own pattern and decoration as described on page* 17.

Assembling: The frame is always fastened to the underside (i.e., the undecorated side) of the sail. For the small kites the frame is simply glued straight onto the paper. Cover the shiny side of the kite sticks with glue, mark their position on the sail, and stick them to the paper. Leave to dry.

The larger frames are bound together with linen thread. Put some glue at the point where the sticks will intersect, bind the thread around, and tie it fast. Put a little more glue on top and allow to dry. The binding of the different parts of the frame is explained in detail for each kite.

Small kites can be decorated before the frame is stuck to the sail. But with the more complicated models, where the sticks have to be bound and glued, the decoration is best left until the end.

The tail can be made out of crepe paper or wrapping paper. Cut out several strips about 1-inch wide from the roll before you undo it (as if you were slicing an ice-cream roll). The tail is designed to stabilize the kite and hold it facing into the wind. The stronger the wind, the heavier the tail needs to be. We have suggested an approximate tail length for all the kites that require them, but you may have to adjust it according to the strength of the wind or any changes in wind conditions while the kite is in the air.

If the kite spins around in the air, it is an indication that the tail is not heavy enough, and you will need to make it longer.

If the kite refuses to take off, the tail is too heavy. Remove one or two strips or shorten it.

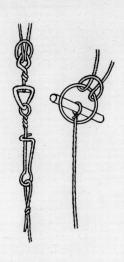

Two ways of attaching the bridle (top string) to the handline (bottom string):
Left: *using a swivel fishing hook.*
Right: *using a small piece of wood and a curtain ring.*

The bridle is made of thin twine or linen thread on the very small kites. It should be at least two and a half times as long as the distance between the two points where it is fastened to the frame. The bridle is attached to the different points on the frame as indicated, and also to a ring (curtain ring for example), approximately halfway between them, that links it to the handline. A swivel fishing hook (preferably with a safety clip) or a small piece of wood can be slipped into this ring, thus enabling the flier to unfasten the line very swiftly whenever necessary.

The tilt of the kite: This is determined by the angle of the bridle, but it is impossible to indicate in advance exactly what this angle should be. The best method is simply to find out by trial and error, moving the ring up and down the bridle until you find the right spot. Once you have found the correct position, you will not need to change it again. Any further adjustments can be made by altering the weight and length of the tail.

To sum up: The bridle affects the tilt of the kite, and the tail affects its behavior in different conditions and winds.

The handline is made of thin twine (or linen thread for the smallest of the kites). The line is wound round a reel; various types of hand reels are described on page 77.

1: *The bamboo is split in half.*
2: *The kite sticks are bound together.*
3–4: *The notched edges of the paper are folded over and stuck down.*
5: *The frame is complete.*

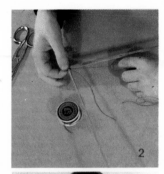

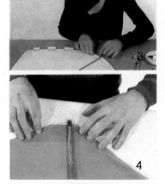

If you have never made a kite before, follow the instructions for each model very carefully. If you want to add a personal touch, you can always do so in your choice of decoration. Once you are familiar with the technique and fully understand the relationship between sail and frame and the different adjustments to be made, you will be able to start designing your own models.

The first kites in the book are the easiest to make and to fly.

Hit the headlines:

Kites
made from
newspapers

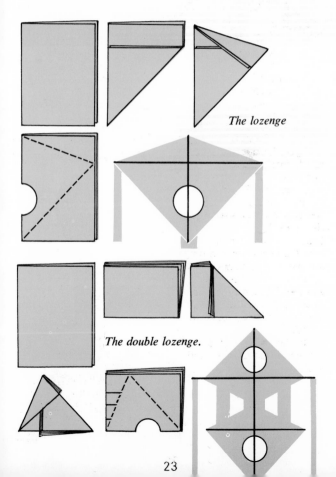

The lozenge

The double lozenge.

23

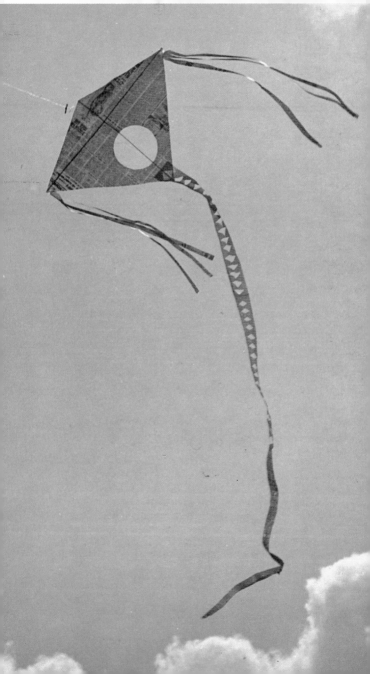

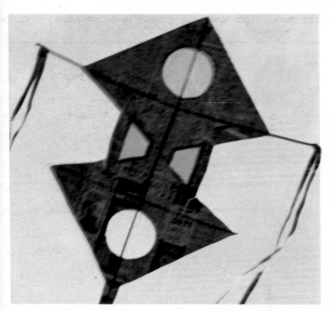

These kites are made without a pattern using sheets of newspaper folded in different ways. You can make your kite most attractive by adding fringes or scalloped edges or cutting out holes and making colored "windows" out of cellophane paper or transparent candy wrappers. These will show up to great advantage in the sunlight. You can also alter the shape of the sail or invent your own shapes to fit the same basic frames, provided the kite is always roughly the same size as the original.

The lozenge

Frame: Sticks 1/8 × 1/12 inch.

Sail: A sheet of newspaper folded as in the diagram at the top of page 23.

Tail: One strip of newspaper 6 feet 6 inches long with holes cut out of it, plus three little extra strips on either side.

The double lozenge

Frame: Sticks 1/8 × 1/12 inch. The horizontal stick protrudes 2 inches on either side of the kite.

Sail: A sheet of newspaper folded as in the diagram at the bottom of page 23.

The owl

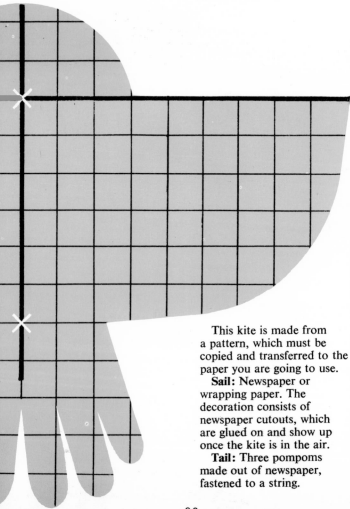

This kite is made from
a pattern, which must be
copied and transferred to the
paper you are going to use.
Sail: Newspaper or
wrapping paper. The
decoration consists of
newspaper cutouts, which
are glued on and show up
once the kite is in the air.
Tail: Three pompoms
made out of newspaper,
fastened to a string.

The slightest puff of wind sends them hurtling forward

Flying saucers

These kites take off very easily and are therefore good ones to choose if you want some practice in launching your kite. There is no bridle on the flying saucers, and the handline can either be fastened directly to the kite, or if you want to be able to remove it easily, make a loop and slip a piece of wood through instead.

28

Flying saucers are traditionally flat and round but you can vary the shape (i.e. oval, hexagonal, square, star-shaped, a face, an insect, etc.) provided the overall size of the kite remains the same and the shape is always symmetrical.

The blue moon and the pink moon

Frame: Sticks 1/8 × 1/12 inch.

Sail: Paper should be lightweight, but not too flimsy. Page of a notebook, lightweight drawing paper, wrapping paper, newspaper.

Tail: Four strips of crepe paper 10 feet long. Two small strips can be added on either side.

The fish

This kite is built on the flying saucer principle, but with the addition of two extra sticks 1/12 × 1/16 inch thick which support the tail. The body is made in shiny paper and the fins and the tail in crepe paper, which is both light and decorative.

Tail: Six miniature paper fish, ranging in size from 4 1/4 to 2 1/2 inches are glued to a string 6 feet 6 inches long.

The flower

Sail: Draw the circle and use a T-square to divide it into six equal parts of

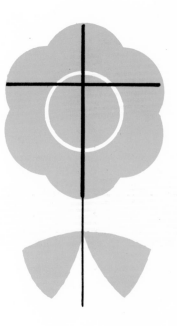

60 degrees each; draw in the petals.

Tail: Use a piece of thin string with three twists of paper attached to it at 6-inch intervals, plus six strips of paper 5/8 inch wide and 6 feet 6 inches long.

A phantom wafting through the air

The ghost

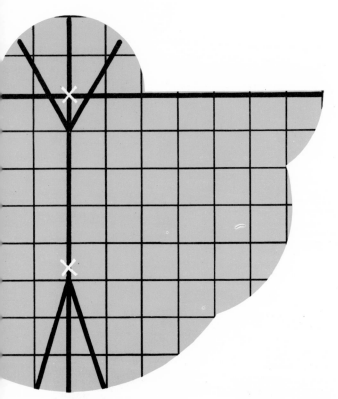

This model is very light and flimsy and can be made either with a tail as in the photo on the previous page, or without one, in which case you will need to elongate the slanting sides a little.

Frame: Horizontal and vertical sticks 1/6 × 1/8 inch. Sticks for the head 1/12 × 1/16 inch, sticks for tail 1/8 × 1/12 inch.

Sail: Crepe paper.

Tail: 3 strips, 3 feet 3 inches long.

Aeroprisms

Small paper box kites

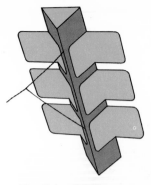

Box kites are constructed in quite a different way from the ones mentioned so far. They are much stronger and more stable. The larger and more complicated models are described at the end of the book.

The aeroprism

This kite is made from a piece of paper that is cut out and then folded into the shape of a triangular box. It is not at all difficult to make.

Frame: The sticks should be as light as possible and 1/12 × 1/16 inch thick— drinking straws or small twigs, for example.

Sail: Page of a notebook, lightweight drawing paper, or wrapping paper. Take a careful look at the pattern before you start. Cut along the continuous white line with a knife, fold the paper along the dotted lines, and glue together as indicated.

Tail: Four strips 1/2 inch wide and 3 feet long.

The flying fish

This fish is constructed in much the same way as the aeroprism, but it is larger and has wings that are glued on as shown in the diagram above. Its curious shape lends itself to all sorts of different forms of decoration.

Frame: Sticks 1/8 × 1/12 inch.

Sail: Lightweight drawing paper or wrapping paper.

Tail: 3 strips, 6 feet long.

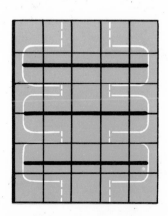

The little airplane

This model consists of two separate cells or boxes and is a little more elaborate than the previous ones. Because it is easy to fly and very stable once in the air, this kite can be used to send up the messengers described on page 86.

Frame: Vertical stick and horizontal sticks 1/6 × 1/8 inch, stick for the box 1/8 × 1/8 inch, slanting sticks 1/12 × 1/12 inch.

Sail: Drawing paper or strong wrapping paper. You can cut out little windows in the wings and stick cellophane paper behind them.

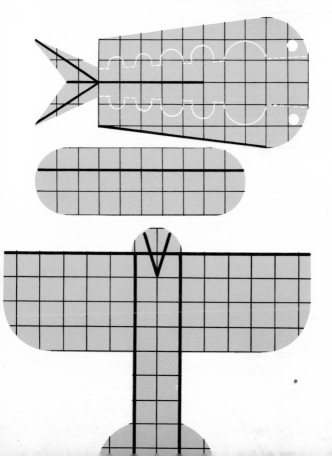

Tail: 3 strips, 6 feet 6 inches long. If the paper used for the sail is not too stiff, the kite will fly just as well without a tail.

Always at home in the sky

Birds

All these kites are light and simple to construct and offer a great deal of scope to anyone with imaginative ideas about decoration. Part of the sail is made in strong paper—lightweight drawing paper, shiny paper, or wrapping paper, and can be decorated, using a felt-tip pen, watercolors or a collage of small pieces of paper. It is a good idea to protect the painted areas with a layer of colorless varnish. The outside edges of the wings and the tail are in crepe paper, which makes the kite lighter and more attractive in flight. The crepe paper is stuck to the underside of the sail with an overlap of 3/8 inch. This part is very fragile and may tear after a little use. A piece of cotton thread glued along the outside edge will help to strengthen it.

All the different bird kites are easy to launch and very spectacular in flight. You may find that real birds will come and investigate them at closer quarters. To make the kites more stable, fasten a length of linen thread to either end of the horizontal stick in order to give it a slight curve.

The hummingbird

Frame: Horizontal and vertical sticks 1/8 × 1/12 inch, slanting sticks 1/12 × 1/16 inch. The vertical stick protrudes in front to form the beak and can be painted.

Tail: Three strips 5/8 inch wide and 3 feet 3 inches long, fastened on either side.

The hummingbird and the sea gull

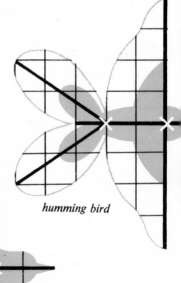

humming bird

sea gull

The sea gull

Frame: Horizontal and vertical sticks $1/8 \times 1/12$ inch, tail stick $1/12 \times 1/16$ inch.

Tail: The small fish (7 inches) that the sea gull pulls along behind it is attached to a string 2 feet 3 inches long. Four other strips 1 foot 8 inches long are joined to this first string.

40

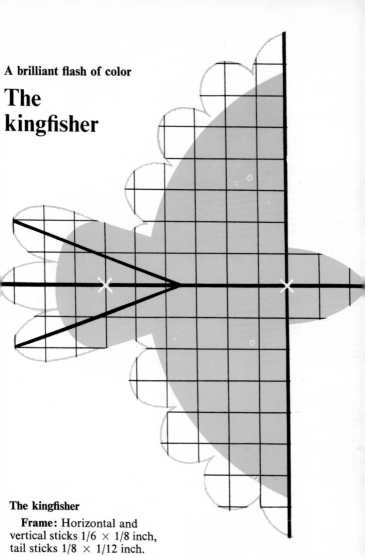

A brilliant flash of color

The kingfisher

The kingfisher

Frame: Horizontal and vertical sticks 1/6 × 1/8 inch, tail sticks 1/8 × 1/12 inch.

Tail: Two strips of crepe paper 6 feet 6 inches long in the center with one strip on either side, and three strips 3 feet 3 inches long on both wings.

Dazzling plumage and a long tail

The
pheasant

Frame: Horizontal and vertical sticks 1/8 × 1/12 inch, head and tail sticks 1/12 × 1/16 inch.

Sail: Cut out an extra 5/8 inch at the top of each wing to form a flap to go over the horizontal stick and keep it in a curved position. Make a series of small nicks in this flap. Glue the stick to the sail,

giving it a slight curve, sticking the flap down over the stick to keep it in place as you do so. Attach first one side and then the other in this way.

Tail: Eight strips 3/8 inch wide. The central strips should be 6 feet 6 inches long and the ones on either side each slightly shorter than the next to give a fanlike effect.

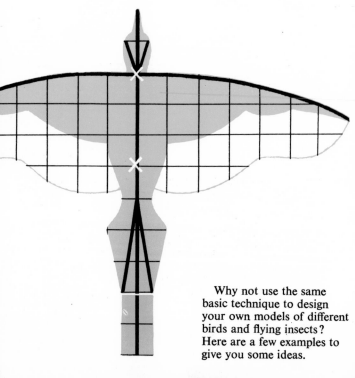

Why not use the same basic technique to design your own models of different birds and flying insects? Here are a few examples to give you some ideas.

44

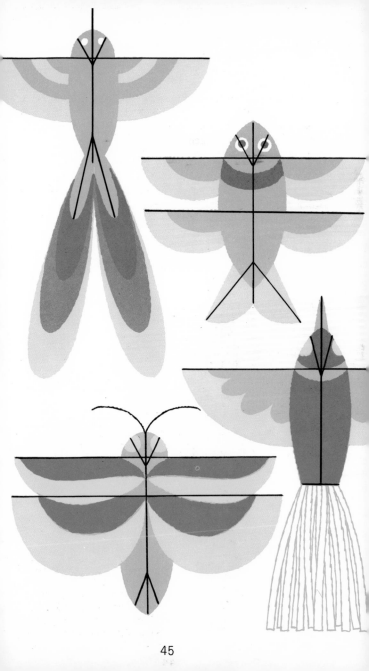

45

An American symbol
The eagle

This is the largest of the bird kites. Being made entirely of strong paper, it is more solid than the others and also more difficult to launch. You will need to attach a string to either end of the wings to give them a definite curve. The stronger the wind, the more pronounced the curve will need to be.

Frame: Horizontal and vertical sticks 1/6 × 1/8 inch, tail sticks 1/8 × 1/12 inch, head sticks 1/12 × 1/16 inch.

Sail: Lightweight drawing paper, painted and varnished. Allow an extra 5/8 inch at the top of each wing for the flap which is to hold the wing stick in a curved position, and follow the same procedure as for the pheasant, page 44.

Tail: Three strips 6 feet 6 inches long.

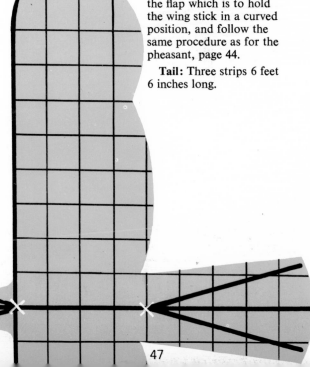

The longest snake in the world

The kite below has a tail 26 yards long. It is made in exactly the same way as the models on the following pages.

Flying snakes

These small kites with their extra-long tails look very spectacular in the air. They are easy to launch in a gentle wind and usually stay up a long time. The frames for these kites are bound together with string rather than being stuck to the sail, and they require a certain amount of care and attention to make.

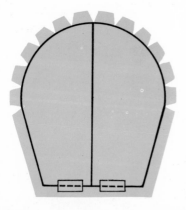

The giant pink cobra

Frame: Vertical stick 1/3 × 1/6 inch thick, or a stick of bamboo 1/3 inch in diameter sliced in half. Lower horizontal stick 1/4 × 1/6 inch. Upper horizontal stick for the arc 5 feet 9 inches long and 1/4 × 1/6 inch thick in the center, planed down evenly on either side until the ends are only 1/8 × 1/12 inch. (The shiny side of the bamboo is turned outward.) Bind one end of the vertical stick to the center of the lower horizontal and the other to the center of the upper horizontal. Now bind the ends of the top horizontal to the ends of the bottom one to form the arc. It does not matter if the curve is not exactly the same as in the diagram, as long as it is symmetrical.

Sail: Strong wrapping paper. Place the frame on the wrong side of the paper and draw around the

outline. Remove the frame, cut out the paper, leaving 3/8 inch more all the way round for the flap. Cut off the corners and make a series of nicks in the curved part of the flap. Position the frame on the paper, glue the flap and fold it down over the frame, leaving the bottom part unstuck until the tail is ready. Glue two little rectangular pieces of paper over the lower stick to keep it in place.

Tail: The tail is the most important feature of the kite and flows out behind it with a curious rustling sound. It is made of one sheet of crepe paper 16 yards 1 foot long, which is 15 3/4 inches wide where it joins the kite and becomes progressively narrower, ending in a point.

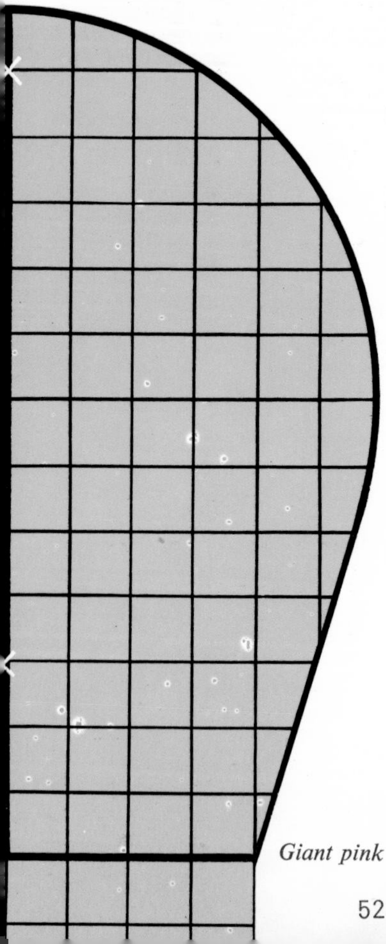

The little blue cobra

Frame: Vertical stick 1/6 × 1/8 inch, horizontal 1/8 × 1/12 inch. Arc 1/8 × 1/12 inch thick and 2 feet 3 1/2 inches long. Bind the two horizontal sticks to either end of the vertical one as for the cobra. Stretch both ends of the upper horizontal to achieve the same curve as in the diagram.

Sail: Crepe paper or lightweight wrapping paper. Fitted in the same way as for the cobra.

Tail: Crepe paper, 11 yards long.

Giant pink cobra.

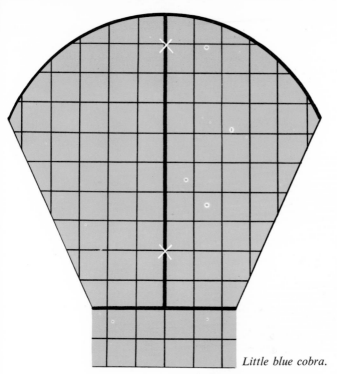

Little blue cobra.

The grass snake

This very small snake, which is shown in diagram form only, has the same characteristics as the others, but is much simpler to make because the head is in the shape of a flying saucer.

Frame: Two sticks
1/8 × 1/12 inch, crossed and glued together.

Sail: Thick wrapping paper or drawing paper.

Tail: Crepe paper,
7 yards 2 feet long.

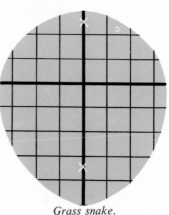

Grass snake.

53

The Polynesian bird in flight.

From the Pacific

The Polynesian bird

This model is a copy of a Polynesian kite. The original was made out of banana leaves and had a wing-span of 11 feet. Our kite is not on such an ambitious scale, but it is very impressive in flight, hovering almost motionless in the air, wings arched as if it were some huge bird of prey.

Frame: The wing stick is 5 feet 4 inches long. It is 1/3 × 1/6 inch thick in the center and must be filed down progressively until the two ends are 1/8 × 1/8 inch thick. All the other sticks are 1/6 × 1/8 inch. To give the wing stick its curve, first soak it for five minutes in cold water to make the wood supple; then, holding it over a candle flame, bend it slowly to the desired shape, checking carefully with the pattern as you do so. For the kite to be perfectly balanced, the two curves must be exactly identical.

Sail: Use thick wrapping paper. Cut out the wings, leaving 3/8 inch along the top of the flap. Be careful to make the curve at the end of each wing as accurate as possible since this curve is an important guide for the wing stick. Glue the different parts of the frame to the wings in this order: first the vertical stick, then the tail sticks, and last of all the wing stick.

The bridle: This is attached to the kite at three separate points. Fix the string to the two highest points first. As in all the models, the distance between these two points is just under half the length of the kite. The lower part of the bridle is longer than the distance

between the two highest points, so that once in the air the kite tilts slightly backward.

A piece of thin twine holds the wings in place. This twine is fastened to the wing stick on the underside of the kite at two points about 1 foot 8 inches from the center. The angle of the curve depends on the strength of the wind. The stronger the wind, the more pronounced the curve should be.

On tailless kites the curve controls the kite in the same way that the tail does on other kites. If at first you have difficulty mastering this technique, you can always add a small crepe-paper tail to any of the kites described here.

Hovering motionless

The
Siamese owl

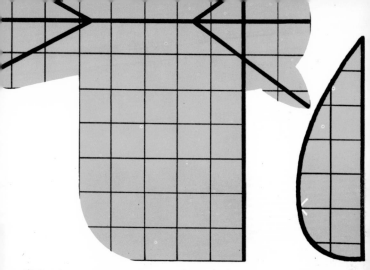

This kite is extremely light and will take off even when there is very little wind. It is also very stable. The bridle has been replaced by a movable panel to which the handline can be fastened directly.

Frame: Vertical and horizontal sticks 1/6 × 1/8 inch. Head and tail sticks 1/8 × 1/12 inch. Glue on the horizontal stick last of all.

Sail: Crepe paper. Any form of decoration must be very light; the colored pieces of paper you see here have been stuck on side by side and not one on top of the other.

Movable panel: Stick and curved section 1/8 × 1/12 inch, shiny side turned outward. A piece of basket cane or rattan can be used for the curved section. Cut out the paper, leaving an extra 3/8 inch all the way around for the flap. Glue the frame to the paper, cut notches in the flap, and stick it down. If you want to hide the flap, stick another piece of paper the same size and shape but without a flap on top of the original one. The movable panel is attached to the vertical stick in two places. Use some linen thread; wind it round and round with the aid of a needle, without pulling it too tight. The two joins must be flexible enough to serve as hinges.

The bird man

This kite is constructed in the same way as the other bird kites, but is slightly heavier as there is no crepe paper border.

You can, however, make the kite a little lighter by cutting out "windows" in the shape of feathers all the way around the wings and sticking crepe paper behind them. This will look very effective from a distance.

Frame: Horizontal and vertical sticks 1/6 × 1/8 inch. Slanting sticks for the tail 1/8 × 1/12 inch, slanting sticks for the head 1/12 × 1/16 inch.

Sail: Wrapping paper or paper for covering notebooks.

Tail: A length of thin string with one pompom attached 2 feet 3 1/2 inches from the kite and another 11 1/2 inches lower down, together with three strips each 6 feet 6 inches long.

The illustration of this kite on page 20 shows how the bridle should be attached.

61

For a moonlit night

Isis's crescent

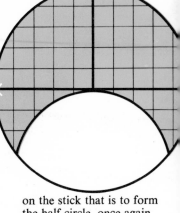

This kite is in fact an adaptation of a Hawaiian kite, but we have given it this name because the crescent moon is one of the symbols of the ancient Egyptian goddess Isis.

Frame: Stick for outside edge of circle, 1/6 × 1/12 inch thick and 5 feet 3 inches long; small half-circle stick 1/8 × 1/12 inch thick and 1 foot 10 inches long; horizontal and vertical sticks 1/6 × 1/8 inch.

Sail: Japanese vellum, which is varnished once the kite is finished, or tracing paper. First of all mark the places where the circle and the horizontal and vertical sticks are to go on paper. Tie together the two ends of the stick for the circle. Coat it in glue and place it in position on the paper. Leave it to dry and then cut out the paper around it. Now put the horizontal stick in place and fasten both ends to the circle, using thread and a needle to pierce the paper. The two ends should protrude to make this easier. Glue

on the stick that is to form the half circle, once again binding both ends to the circle in the same way. Tie the vertical stick in position and cut out the paper from inside the small half circle.

Tail: Four strips 13 feet long.

Bridle: This is what is known as a three-leg bridle. It consists of two separate pieces of thin twine, which are attached to the kite at three different points (marked by white crosses on the diagram). The lower section of the bridle runs horizontally between the two lowest points on the kite; the upper section runs vertically from the highest point on the sail to the middle of the lower bridle. Adjust the vertical section to give the kite the required tilt.

Geometry gone wild

The hexagon

Below: *Cloth version of the hexagon: The string is threaded through the hemmed slots; the sticks are held in place by small pockets sewn to the corners.*

This is one example of a geometrical kite. The other ones (illustrated in diagram form only on page 65) are all built in the same way as the hexagon. The design of these geometrical kites makes them extremely strong, and they can be constructed on a very large scale without any problem.

Frame: Three poplar sticks or bamboo canes 3/8 × 1/6 inch. The horizontal stick is 2 feet 6 inches long and the other two are 3 feet long. Make a notch 3/8 inch from the end of each one to take the string. Bind the three sticks together in the middle; the slanting ones can be more or less far apart as long as the overall symmetry of the kite is maintained.

Take a piece of thin twine long enough to go around the whole of the outside and, starting from the right-hand top corner, tie the string to each notch in turn, using a clove hitch, as illustrated below.

Check that the first two sides of the hexagon are the

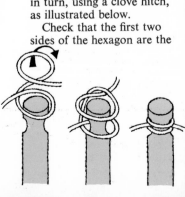

same length before knotting the string to the end of each stick all the way round.

Sail: Strong wrapping paper. Place the frame, with the shiny or curved side down, on top of the paper. Trace the outline of the kite onto the paper, allowing 5/8 inch more for the flap. Remove the frame and cut out the paper, snipping off the corners as you go. Put the frame back in place, glue the flap all the way round, and fold it down over the string.

Glue some small rectangular pieces of paper to each of the kite sticks to prevent the wind from blowing the kite inside out when you are moving it from one place to another.

The tail: A strip of scalloped crepe paper 13 feet long and 2 1/2 inches wide, folded and glued to a piece of string with a big pompom on the end. The string to which it is attached should form a triangle equal in height to half the height of the kite.

A three-leg bridle: A must for this kite. It is attached to the top of the two slanting sticks and to the center of the kite.

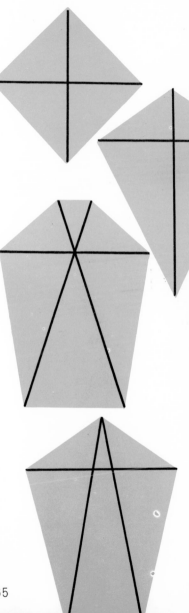

The pear-shaped kite

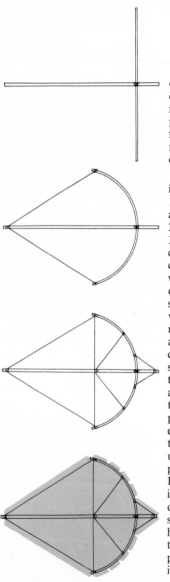

This is the most traditional of all the models and is often seen in eighteenth- or nineteenth-century paintings. Being light, it flies extremely well, but it needs to be made with great care and precision.

Frame: The vertical stick is a piece of bamboo 1/3 inch in diameter. The arc is made from a stick 2 feet 6 inches long and 3/16 × 1/8 thick at its central point. If possible, choose a piece of wood on which the knots are evenly distributed, then trim both sides down progressively with a knife until the stick measures 1/12 × 1/12 inch at either end. Bind the center of the horizontal stick that is to form the arc to the vertical one, leaving a projecting tip as shown in the diagram. Fasten two pieces of thin twine to either end of this stick and tighten each one in turn until the stick is bent in a perfectly symmetrical curve. It does not need to be identical to the one in the diagram. Tie the two supporting strings, the horizontal string, and the two strings from the small projecting tip of the kite in place.

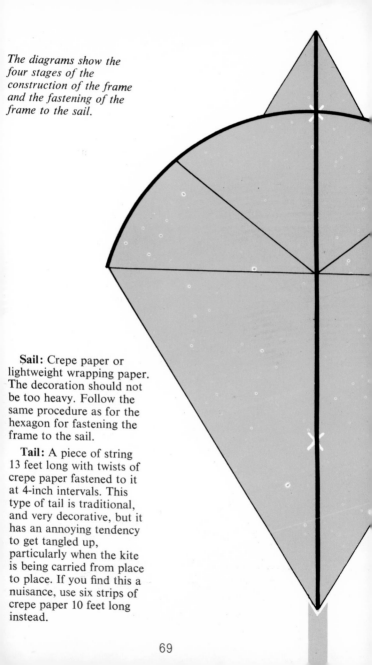

The diagrams show the
four stages of the
construction of the frame
and the fastening of the
frame to the sail.

Sail: Crepe paper or
lightweight wrapping paper.
The decoration should not
be too heavy. Follow the
same procedure as for the
hexagon for fastening the
frame to the sail.

Tail: A piece of string
13 feet long with twists of
crepe paper fastened to it
at 4-inch intervals. This
type of tail is traditional,
and very decorative, but it
has an annoying tendency
to get tangled up,
particularly when the kite
is being carried from place
to place. If you find this a
nuisance, use six strips of
crepe paper 10 feet long
instead.

Defying the clouds

The Indian chief

This is the first of the cloth kites, but all the models we give can just as well be made in tough brown wrapping paper.

Sail: The material is folded in two and the sail cut out allowing 1 1/4 inches for the hem at the top and 5/8 inch all the way round. Hem down the sides and decorate the cloth.

Mark the position for the slanting and vertical sticks on the wrong side of the cloth and sew on three pockets at the bottom to hold the ends of the sticks in

place, and three small slots to secure them halfway up. Fasten two tabs, one on either side of the kite, at the top, on the right side of the material, and slip a metal ring (such as a curtain ring) or a loop of string over each one (see diagram on page 74 for the Russian giant). Now make a hem along the top to house the horizontal stick, leaving a gap of 4 inches unstitched in the middle.

Frame: Horizontal and vertical sticks are in bamboo 1/3 inch in diameter. The slanting sticks are half-width bamboos of the same diameter. The cross-stick is 3/16 × 1/8 inch thick. The ends of the horizontal stick should protrude 1/12 inch on either side of the sail. A notch is made in each one to house the ring. Wind a piece of string around and glue it down to prevent the stick from splitting.

Fit the four main kite sticks, slipping the rings into the prepared notches, and bind them together at the top. Add the cross-stick and bind all five sticks together in the middle (see diagram for the Russian giant).

Decoration: The Indian chief's face and the two shoulder strips are made of strong Bristol board. The braids, made of crepe paper, hang down on either side of the chief's face.

Tail: Three strips of crepe paper 5 feet long on either side, joined together with a pompom. Three strips of crepe paper 6 feet 6 inches long attached to the end of each arm.

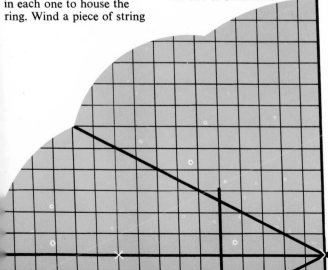

The
Russian
giant

This kite is the largest in the book and can be launched only in a strong wind with at least two people present, one to hold the kite and the other to fly it, preferably with the hand reel attached to his waist and wearing gloves to protect his hands.

Frame: The two horizontals are made from bamboo sticks 1/3 inch in diameter, the two diagonals from bamboos 9/16 inch in diameter. The horizontals should protrude about 3/4 inch beyond the sail on either side. Notch and bind the ends of the horizontals (as for the Indian chief).

Sail: Rectangular, in cloth or very strong brown paper, measuring 4 × 5 feet. Allow 3/4 inch for the hem

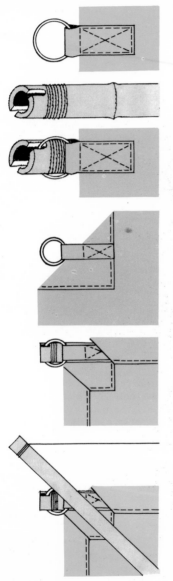

on the two longer sides and 1 1/4 inches on the shorter ones. Sew the two longest hems and decorate the kite. With the wrong side up, fold down the four corners and stitch the tabs in place as shown in the diagram. Now make the shorter hems to house the kite sticks.

Slide the horizontals into the hemmed slots and place the rings in the notched and bound ends of the sticks. Now add the diagonals, first binding them to the horizontals and then tying them together in the middle where they intersect. They should both project 3 inches on one side in order to make it possible to attach a string to them. Use thin twine for all binding.

Thread a string through each of the longer seams, pull it tight, and attach the ends to the horizontals projecting at each corner. Fasten a string between the two projecting ends of the diagonals to give the kite a hollow curve of roughly 4 inches to 6 inches. (As for the Polynesian bird, the curve depends on the strength of the wind.) A rectangular piece of stiff paper attached halfway along this string will help in the wind and provide extra wind resistance.

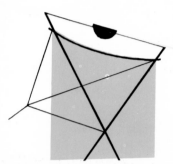

The bridle is attached at three points: to the top of the two slanting sticks and to the center of the kite.

The Bridle: A three-leg one; the top section must be equal in length to the two sides of the triangle formed by the diagonals, the bottom section equal in length to the height of the same triangle.

Tail: 16 yards 1 foot long. Consists of a scalloped strip of crepe paper 4 inches wide, with a string reinforcement and a pompom at the end. The tail is attached by means of a second piece of string anchored to the two bottom corners of the kite itself. The triangle thus formed is the same height as the kite itself.

Hand reels

Here are three very simple versions:
• Four pieces of bamboo approximately 1/3 inch in diameter, two of them 4 inches long and two 7 inches long. Grooves are cut in each of the top two pieces to house the bottom ones and all four are then bound together. Two quarter-width bamboos are crossed and bound on top of the others to give extra support.
• Two wooden handles 1/3 inch in diameter and a small rectangular wooden board 5 × 2 1/2 inches and 3/8 inch thick. The handles are planed down on the side that is to be nailed to the board.
• Two wooden handles 1/3 inch in diameter and two small rectangular boards 6 × 1 1/4 inches and 3/8 inch thick. Use a brace to drill holes for the handles. Nail the handles in place.

Small hand reels.

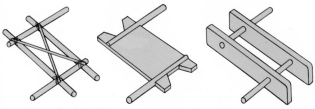

The large hand reel.

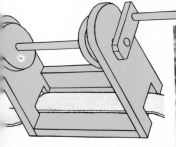

The large hand reel, which can be attached to the flier's belt, is an essential piece of equipment when flying the larger kites. Cut out the different parts from a wooden board 3/8 inch thick. Make the necessary holes with a brace. The handle and the spindle are made from a cylindrical stick 3/8 inch in diameter. The different parts of the support are nailed together. A stop bolt on the side opposite the handle can be slid into a hole, thus jamming the reel. A big fishing reel can also be adapted for use as a hand reel.

A collapsible kite

The cellular airplane

This is one of the simplest of the many box kites and you may want to try your hand at some others, using the diagrams on page 81 as a guide. This particular model is extremely stable and ideally suited for sending messengers up on the handline. The cloth version is collapsible (which makes transport much easier), but the airplane can also be made in tough wrapping paper.

Sail: The cloth is folded in half and cut out with a hem allowance of 3/8 inch for the sides and 1 inch for the top and bottom.

Mark the position of the vertical sticks on the right side of the cloth. Sew four tabs and rings on either side at the top and bottom and four more at the far ends of the hems. Sew down the top and bottom hems on the wrong side of the cloth.

Cells: Cut out two rectangles 21 × 10 inches plus 3/8 inch for the hem all the way round. Hem down the long sides of each rectangle. On the right side of the sail sew on two reinforcements measuring 3/4 × 1 5/8 inches as indicated in the diagram on page 80. Make two little eyelets on either side of each reinforcement and oversew the edges. Fold the cells along the middle and stitch them 3/4 inch from the fold

to make a slot. Cut out two more slots, making them 3/4 inch wide and the same length as the height of the kite (not counting the hem allowance). Now make hems along the short sides. Stitch the slots to the right side of the cloth so that they straddle the line for the vertical sticks. Stitch the two cells in position at the same time (see diagram).

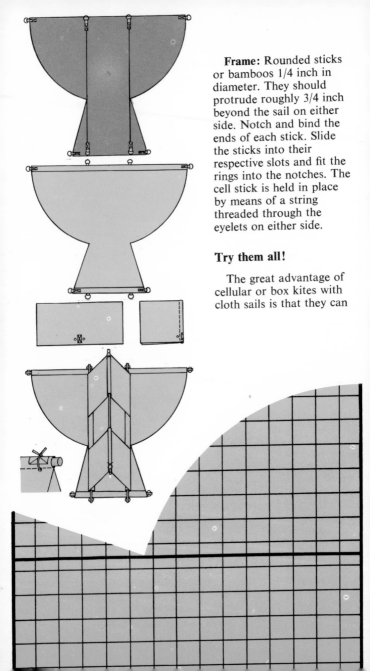

Frame: Rounded sticks or bamboos 1/4 inch in diameter. They should protrude roughly 3/4 inch beyond the sail on either side. Notch and bind the ends of each stick. Slide the sticks into their respective slots and fit the rings into the notches. The cell stick is held in place by means of a string threaded through the eyelets on either side.

Try them all!

The great advantage of cellular or box kites with cloth sails is that they can be dismantled and they do not tear easily; once in the air, they are very stable and fly exceptionally well. They are, however, much more complicated to make than other kites and should really only be undertaken by very expert kite-makers.

You may like to try your hand at making some of the kites shown on this page, using the same technique as for the airplane. If you use thick wrapping paper instead of cloth, you will find it much easier, but, of course, the kite cannot be taken apart once finished.

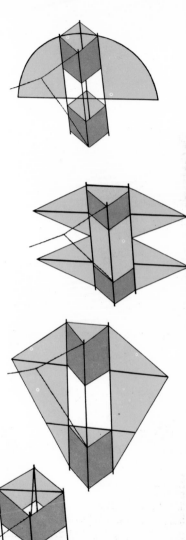

81

Myth and magic combine in...

The mighty Chinese dragon

This traditional kite can be made as large or as small as you like (anything up to 20 yards in length!). And there is nothing to stop you from decorating it quite differently and making a fearsome dragon breathing forth fire and smoke. Once in the air, this kite moves along with a curious rippling motion, rather like a giant centipede. This particular model consists of nine separate disks attached one behind the other in order of size.

Sail: Lightweight wrapping paper.

Frame: The circumference of each disk is made of a length of rattan 1/8 inch in diameter. The cross-sticks are bamboos 1/8 × 1/12 inch thick. The disk for the head is 15 inches in diameter; the other disks measure: 14, 13 1/2, 13, 12 1/2, 12, 11 1/2, 11 and 10 1/2 inches respectively, i.e. each consecutive disk is 1/2 inch less in diameter. Trace the first circle onto the wrong side of the sail. Take a piece of cane the same length as the circumference of the circle and bind the ends together. Glue the cane to the sail, leave to dry, and cut the paper away around the frame (no flaps are needed). Cross the two cross-sticks in the middle and bind them to the cane, using thread and a needle to pierce the paper. The vertical sticks should protrude very slightly. The horizontal ones should protrude 2 inches on either side so that the balancers can be made of either real feathers or imitation ones in

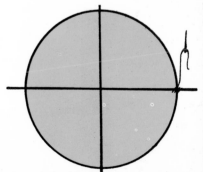

83

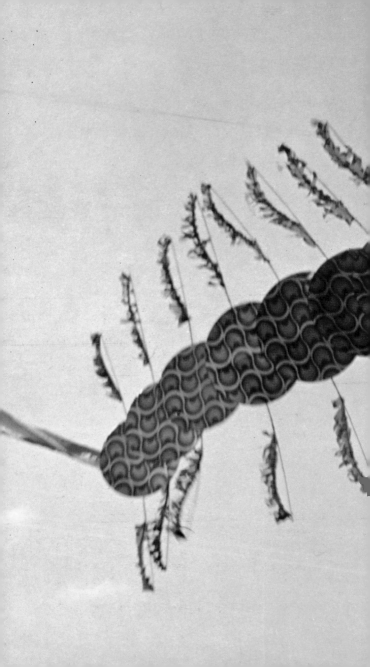

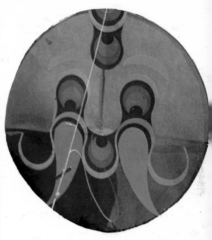

crepe paper stuck to a piece of bamboo 14 1/2 inches long (see photo). The length of the balancers should be decreased progressively in relation to the size of the disks.

Assembly: The disks are joined together by three strings knotted and glued to the ends of the horizontal stick and to the top of the vertical stick on every disk. The distance between the first two disks is 11 1/2 inches, between the next two 11 inches, and so on, i.e., 1/2 inch less each time.

Tail: Three strips of crepe paper 3 feet 3 inches long attached to the frame of the last disk.

Messengers

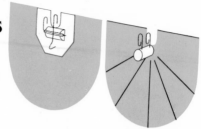

Messengers are a type of secondary kite that can be fastened to the handline once the kite is in the air and, with the aid of the wind, moved up as far as the kite itself or any object attached to the line lower down.
You can use a messenger to send up a Chinese lantern or a flashlight to help you find your way on a dark night. Messengers can also be used, as their name suggests, to drop messages or even bags of confetti or a parachute. Find a wide open space with a steady wind blowing and choose a stable kite (paper or cloth box kite) to send up your first messenger.

The Bird

This is the simplest model of all. It has a wingspan of 1 foot and is made out of drawing paper. Reinforce the underside of the bird's wings with a small stick 1/16 or 1/2 inch wide. Stick on two strips of crepe paper 1 foot 8 inches long for the tail.

The Sail

This model in lightweight wrapping paper can be used to release a parachute. It is reinforced on the wrong side with small sticks and on the right side with a piece of drawing paper. Glue a cork with two paper clips stuck into it to the underside of the sail, where it will act as a guide and keep the messenger moving smoothly up the line. Cut a second cork in half, force a straightened paper clip through it with an elastic band attached, and stick this cork to the top of the sail. Another paper clip or hairpin is slipped through the elastic band as shown in the diagram, and the parachute fastened to it. Now tie a small piece of wood or bamboo quite high up the handline using a clove hitch. When the sail encounters this obstacle, the hairpin springs back, releasing the parachute.

86

The swivel sail

This more complicated and much more solid version of the sail can be used to pull heavier weights than either of the messengers already mentioned. The sail itself is made of turkey red cotton. Cut out an equilateral triangle with sides 15 3/4 inches long, plus a 3/4-inch allowance for the hems. Sew down the hems, leaving the corners free and making a gap 1 1/4 inches long half way up one of the sides. Fit three sticks or bamboos 2 inches in diameter into the hems and slide a ring of bamboo halfway along one of the sticks to coincide with the 1 1/4-inch opening in the hem. The guide will be screwed to the sail by means of this ring.

The guide is made of a smooth, hollow length of bamboo 1/2 inch in diameter. Cut one piece 2 3/4 inches long and make two notches in it (diagram 1). Now attach this bamboo to a second one 8 1/2 inches long by means of two pieces of wire, one of which must be bent into a hook to go over the handline (diagram 2). A second hook made in the same way is fastened to the far end of the longer bamboo. Insert a length of wire first into the long bamboo and then into the short one so that it slides freely (diagram 3). Now screw the guide to the sail (diagram 4). A small ring with a string attached to it to hold the sail at right angles to the guide is slipped over the sliding wire in the shorter bamboo and held in position in the first of the two notches. The parachute is held in place in the same way in the second notch. When the messenger encounters the obstacle on the line, the sliding wire is forced back, releasing the parachute and the string anchoring the sail to the guide simultaneously. The sail swivels round and round, and as it no longer offers any wind resistance, both guide and sail slide back down the handline.

The parachute

The parachute is made of silk or nylon, or some other very fine material. Cut out a circle 14 inches in diameter, sew a small ring to the center of it, hem the outside edge, and attach eight strings 10 inches long to the hem, joining them together farther down with a piece of cellophane and knotting the ends. The parachutist is made out of a piece of drawing paper 2 1/2 inches long wrapped around a cork. Put some

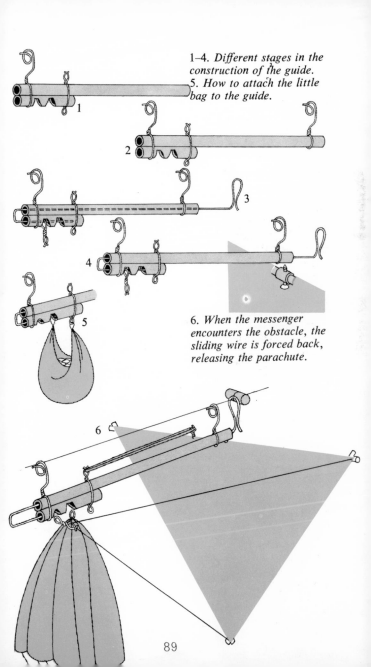

1–4. *Different stages in the construction of the guide.*
5. *How to attach the little bag to the guide.*

6. *When the messenger encounters the obstacle, the sliding wire is forced back, releasing the parachute.*

89

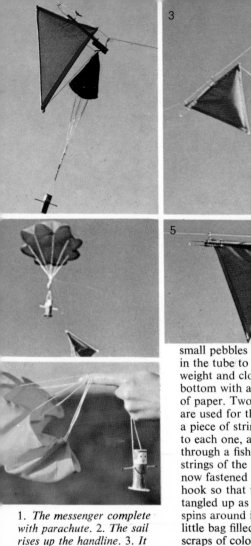

5

1. *The messenger complete with parachute.* 2. *The sail rises up the handline.* 3. *It encounters the obstacle on the line.* 4. *The parachute is released.* 5. *The sail swivels round and round and slides back down.* 6. *The parachute hits the ground.*

small pebbles or some sand in the tube to give extra weight and close off the bottom with a circular piece of paper. Two matchsticks are used for the arms, with a piece of string attached to each one, and threaded through a fishing hook. The strings of the parachute are now fastened to the fishing hook so that they do not get tangled up as the parachute spins around in the air. The little bag filled with small scraps of colored paper can be attached as shown in diagram 5 and will open, scattering its contents far and wide, when the messenger encounters the obstacle on the line.

A parade in the sky

Trains of kites

Several kites attached to a single line.

Any of the kites in this book can be used to lift different objects into the air or to pull objects along on the ground or in water; a single boat or even a small flotilla of boats can be attached to the handline. The very large kites are even strong enough to tow a rubber dinghy with someone inside (make sure the person knows how to swim first!). On a sandy beach or some other smooth surface a large kite will pull a small cart or sled quite easily.

Sometimes a train of smaller kites is more effective than one large one. The total surface area is the same, but the kites are easier to handle and to launch. Either they can be attached one behind the other, using the same technique as for the Chinese dragon, with strings running from one to the next and only one line, or, alternatively, they can be fastened separately, each by an individual line, to different points on the handline of the first kite. In this case, the kites are launched one after the other and not all at once. Remember that all the kites in a train of kites must be the same, so that the surface area of each one is identical.

What about a whistling kite? Fasten some whistles to the kite with the mouth ends facing into the wind.

A train of kites.

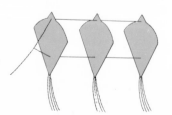

Some words on kite height

How high can it fly?

It is possible to estimate the height of your kite without elaborate calculations. You need a flat open space and two friends to help you. First of all make yourself a simple surveyor's instrument using an ordinary 45-degree drafting triangle or a square of light cardboard cut in half along the diagonal. Make a hole in the right-angled corner of the triangle and nail it loosely to a straight piece of wood. When you lift the triangle up by means of this piece of wood, it should swing freely on the nail so that its own weight keeps the base permanently horizontal, irrespective of the angle at which the stick is held. If you are using a cardboard triangle you may need to glue a small stick along the base of it to give it extra weight.

Once you have launched the kite, take up your positions as follows: the first person holds the kite, the second one stands directly underneath it, and the third one stands to one side with the T square held at eye level, looking up toward the kite along the diagonal and changing his position until the kite appears in the extension of this line. At this point the height of the kite above the ground is equal to the distance between the second and third person, plus the height of the T square from the ground (see diagram).

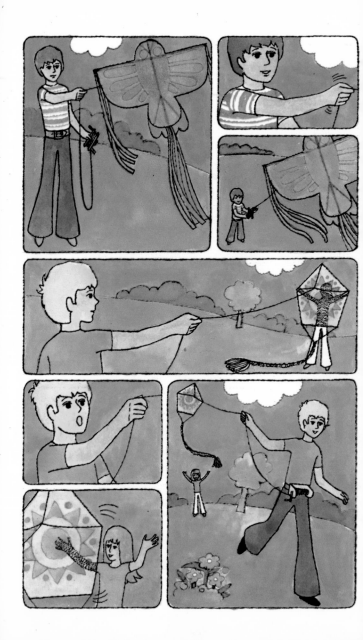

Last but not least

Launching your kite

Ideal conditions for launching are a large open space like a field or a beach, with a steady wind blowing from one direction without any sudden gusts or squalls. Avoid any spots such as clearings or riverbanks, where the wind is apt to change suddenly. The small kites will be much easier to launch in a gentle wind and may well tear if the wind is too strong. Big kites, on the other hand, will only take off in a reasonably strong wind. Stand with your back to the wind and unwind several yards of line, holding the kite at arm's length and pulling on the line gently. With a larger kite ask a friend to help you by standing a little way off with the kite held out in front of him, letting go when you give the signal. A kite should never be thrown into the air, but simply released when the wind is strong enough to lift it.

Be very careful how you handle your kite and try to avoid any sudden movement once it is in the air. If a particularly violent gust of wind causes it to lose height, unwind a little of the line to give it extra play. Never pull it along on the ground once it has come down or you will tear it.

If you want to bring the kite down in a hurry, make the line fast or give it to someone to hold, put your arm over the line, and run toward the kite. Always take a pair of scissors, some glue, cellophane tape, and two or three strips of crepe paper with you for on-the-spot emergencies.

A WORD OF WARNING: Never fly a kite near a railway line or a busy road. If the kite comes down suddenly in front of car, it may cause an accident. Never fly a kite in stormy weather because it will sometimes act as a lightning conductor (with you as the earth!).

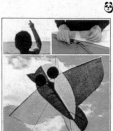